better together*

*This book is best read together, grownup and kid.

a akidsco.com

a
kids
book
about

a kids book about school shootings

for survivors

by Crystal Woodman Miller

a kids book about

Printed in the United States of America.

A Kids Book About books are available online: *akidsco.com*

To share your stories, ask questions, or inquire about bulk purchases (schools, libraries, and nonprofits), please use the following email address: *hello@akidsco.com*

ISBN: 978-1-953955-84-5

Designed by Duke Stebbins
Edited by Emma Wolf

Interested in bringing Crystal Miller
to your school or event? Visit crystalwoodmanmiller.com

For all the kids who have felt the impact
and heartache of a mass shooting and
wondered if there was hope.

This book is for you, because there is
always hope to be found.

Intro

We live in a world where school shootings are not only possible, but have seemingly become commonplace. And when the unthinkable happens at your own kid's school, knowing how to respond may feel impossible.

There is no easy explanation or quick fix for suffering so deep. However, what you can offer a grieving kid who has survived a school shooting is your presence. You can talk less and listen more, creating space for them to safely process the shock, fear, anger, worry, confusion, panic, hopelessness (and whatever else they're experiencing), and ask the hard questions. You can also model what it looks like to choose courage in a dangerous world—which is no small task. The good news is, you are not alone in this pursuit.

As a survivor of a school shooting, I have spent the last 23 years learning what can help in healing from this trauma. I wish this book were not necessary, but I want you to know you are part of a community who understands and sees you. My hope is to open a dialogue between you and your kid as they embark on a long journey toward healing, which I am confident is possible.

Let us move forward in hope together!

Hey, I'm Crystal.

I grew up in Littleton, Colorado, and went to Columbine High School

When I was 16 years old, there was a shooting at my school.

For 7 ½ minutes, I waited
and wondered what
it might feel like to die.

I was confused and so afraid.

I thought of all the
things I wanted in life,
and in that moment,
I doubted if they
would ever happen.

Things like:

hugging my parents again,
going to college,
becoming a teacher,
and becoming a mom.

It's hard to explain this feeling
to people who have never
experienced it.

But this is a book for those who have survived a school shooting.

You are the ones I want to speak to right now.

And I want you to know this...

I’m here. I see you.

You are valued. You are loved.

And, I'm proud of you.

I want you to know you did everything you could, even if you don’t believe that right now.

The truth is, something like this should have never happened to you or to anyone.

A school shooting is **wrong**.

People dying at school is **wrong**.

Someone coming into your school

to hurt and kill people is **wrong**.

It's unfair.

And it’s not your fault.

No one did anything to deserve this.

Whatever you were able to do
when the shooter was at your school,
you were brave and courageous.

You may have felt a lot of things about what you've experienced that I've felt too...

a lot of feelings,
no feelings at all,
or feelings that
don't make sense.

Feeling grateful to be alive,
but also guilty that you survived when others didn't.*

**This is often called survivor's guilt.*

Wanting to be around people,
and at the same time,
wanting to be alone.

Wanting to cry...

Wanting to eat...

Wanting to sleep...

but your eyes staying dry.

but feeling sick to your stomach.

but nightmares are
keeping you awake.

I put so much pressure on myself to heal and get better.

But as time went on, I realized this type of pain won't ever go away completely.

In some ways,
it stays with you
for the rest of your life.

You've experienced grief.

And trauma.

And deep emotional pain.

Anything you feel as a result of that is normal, completely human, and not weird at all.

What really matters is that you don't avoid or push away those feelings as they come.

This **doesn't** mean you should
pretend you're happy
when you're not or
force yourself to move on
before you're ready.

What it **does** mean is that
when a feeling shows up,
whatever it is,

let it come,

don't walk away from it, and
don't hide it away in the darkness.

Ignoring what happened
to you doesn't work.

I wanted to pretend
the shooting at my school
never happened.

I wished I could go back
to the person I was before.

And even though we can't do that, I can tell you there is joy and life ahead.

You may not see hope and light right now,

but I am here to

believe it for you

until you can believe it for yourself.

Be proud of the small steps you take every day to find hope.

Living your life, breathing, and getting through each day is enough right now.

And little by little, light will start to replace the darkness you feel.

When the shock began to wear off, I would catch myself laughing and smiling and feel so guilty.

How could I laugh when some of my classmates could never laugh again?

I want you to know
that **living your life**,
continuing to grow and learn,
and **finding reasons to laugh again**...

are beautiful ways to push against the fear and honor your friends, classmates, grownups and teachers who are no longer with you.

Talk about them too.

People can get uncomfortable
talking about people
who have died.

Share your favorite stories
about them.

Laugh about the jokes
they told you.

Remember them because
their lives mattered and
they mattered to you.

You have the ability
to have

a good

life.

Here are some things that may bring healing on this journey...

1.

Get the help you need
and ask those you trust
to support you.

Be in community.

We were made to be with people,
so please don't isolate yourself.

2.

Take time to be alone when you need it, but return to the people who love you most and are committed to your healing process.

In this space, we learn to trust others again.

3.

Keep telling and retelling your story.

The more I did that, the less control my emotions had over me.

4.

I learned that when you stop hiding the things you feel—no matter how awful they may seem—and bring them into the light, they lose the ability to be so scary.

5.

One of the things that helped me get through was my faith in God.

It may be that for you too, but it doesn't have to be.

What matters is that you trust in the healing process and find a way to share your feelings, not hide them away.

6.

A good counselor and trauma-informed therapy were also significant tools in my healing.

Trauma-informed therapy* means an expert worked with me using my own experiences and pain to help me heal.

**There are SO many different kinds of therapy out there! Check out the resource page in the back of this book for some examples.*

7.

Be gentle with yourself.

It may take time to find something that works for you.

8.

Most importantly, whatever your healing journey looks like, don't give up.

Keep showing up for yourself because you are worth it.

I know the world may feel heavy, hard, and out of control—especially for you, right now.

Focus on small steps.

Celebrate getting out of bed in the morning or brushing your teeth.

Give yourself the gift of focusing on you and what you need.

Our world has dangers.

But we can live without fear.

I know you are strong.

I know you are resilient.

I know this

life

is for

you.

This tragedy does not get the last say.

Your friend,
Crystal

Outro

The fact that you've read this book means your kid's mental health and well-being are your highest priorities. I applaud your determination, and I am proud of you for doing this hard work and holding space for your kid. This work will benefit both of you forever.

As you operate and live within this new normal, there will be times that feel like progress, and times that don't. Don't worry, and be patient—it's all part of the process. Healing isn't linear, and it constantly twists and turns on itself. This trauma may also reveal other difficult things for you to process, but keep showing up with honesty and vulnerability. It's OK for kids to see your feelings and know you struggle too. Wrap every word you say in reassurance, reminding them they are safe and that together, you will find the best support for the kind of healing they need.

Remember to take care of yourself. You will help your kid more when you prioritize your wellness too. Receive the help others offer, and reach out to professionals who can help you navigate the murky waters of trauma.

This is a new beginning, and you've got this.

SOME TYPES OF THERAPY:

Movement therapy,
where you move and dance to help your brain, heart, and body heal.

Art therapy,
which encourages self-expression through painting, drawing, and other art outlets.

EMDR therapy,
or ***Eye Movement Desensitization and Reprocessing therapy***, where a professional helps reduce the symptoms of your trauma by changing the way your memories are stored in your brain.

Equine therapy,
where being close to horses allows you to feel the powerful connection between animals and humans.

Adventure therapy,
where you do challenging outdoor activities to heal and grow in self-confidence.

Psychodrama,
or experiential, therapy, where you explore your emotions by acting out moments from your past.

Play therapy,
where you get to play as a way of expressing and communicating your feelings.

share your read*

***Tell somebody, post a photo, or give this book away to share what you care about.**

CPSIA information can be obtained
at www.ICGtesting.com
Printed in the USA
LVRC092320040423
743485LV00006B/13

9781953955845

9 781953 955